THE MAN IN THE WHITE SUIT

D1055803

THE MAN IN
THE WHITE SUIT

Nick Drake

BLOODAXE BOOKS

ISBN: 1 85224 488 7

First published 1999 by
Bloodaxe Books Ltd,
P.O. Box 1SN,
Newcastle upon Tyne NE99 1SN.

Bloodaxe Books Ltd acknowledges
the financial assistance of Northern Arts.

Cover printing by J. Thomson Colour Printers Ltd, Glasgow.

Printed in Great Britain by
Cromwell Press Ltd, Trowbridge, Wiltshire.

To Arthur Sale

Acknowledgements

Acknowledgements are due to the editors of the following publications where some of these poems first appeared: *Arvon International Poetry Competition 1989 Anthology* (Arvon, 1991), *The Gregory Anthology 1987-1990* (Hutchinson, 1990), *New Welsh Review*, *New Writing 6* (British Council/Viking 1997), *The Observer Arvon Poetry Collection 1993* (Guardian Newspapers, 1994), *Poetry* (Chicago), *The Poetry Book Society Anthology: 1*, new series (PBS/Hutchinson, 1990), *Poetry Introduction 8* (Faber and Faber, 1993), *Poetry Review* and *Storm*.

Some of these poems were included in a pamphlet collection, *Chocolate and Salt* (Mandeville Press, 1990). 'Cigarettes for Mr Blatny' and 'In Memory of Vincent Cox' won prizes in the Arvon International Poetry Competition in 1989 and 1993. 'The Foley Artist' won second prize in the Cardiff International Poetry Competition in 1996.

I am particularly grateful to the Society of Authors for an Eric Gregory Award given in 1990, and to the Wingate Foundation for a scholarship in 1996.

Special thanks to John Mole, Brenda Manning, Jackie Kay, Liz Lochhead, Paul Rainbow and Dave Stagg.

Contents

'An odd thought strikes me:—
we shall receive no letters in the grave.'
SAMUEL JOHNSON

The Hunt by Night

The coast of Bohemia was every lake,
inland seas on summer maps of wheat;
and the citizens, freed from history
by the winter's Velvet Revolution,
abandoned works and cities to the heat
as if these were the first days of the world.

Crossing the open border from the West,
Mercedes ran the country like a film
on ironic glass and polished bodywork;
out on the lakes, guest-worker families
from Vietnam picknicked in pleasure boats,
an idyll from the old ideology.

At night we sang on benches in the dust:
We all live in a Yellow Submarine,
each drinker's roaring face half-shadowed
by the single naked bulb of a sausage van;
passing cars caught out the revellers
mid-anthem, as their headlights searched the trees.

A Slovak home from Austria declared
his boot was stowed with language books to sell;
a smuggler of English, he would talk
his way into the future, speak the truth,
learn different words for sex; he slammed his beer
and proffered me a gherkin from his jar.

And then the hunt by night, sounding our horns
down blind paths through the woods to a lost park
where sleepers lay, dropped bundles in long grass;
climbed trees, rode roundabouts, danced naked, plunged
our bodies, unpolitical and free,
into the starry carp lake, under a full moon.

Cigarettes for Mr Blatný

His body was folds and twists, his bones seemed doubled
into themselves; I thought of an old toenail
ingrowing, a self-interrogation.

Translation from the Republic's rhetoric
erased his poems from history, cast him up
lunatic and tongue-tied to the strange

language, money, time-tables and clothes
of post-war England's accidental streets:
a question-mark uprooted from its past.

Pencil-sharpener, paper-knife, white sheets;
his daily faith – *my scratchings* – an obscure
testimony true as happiness

torn up by night, confessed again by day;
self-doubt ran through him like a water-mark's
shadow to betray itself in light.

High asylum ceilings were his England,
but the winter-garden was Bohemia-
on-Sea, arcadian, an old abode

with visitors to whom he could declare
not his verse, but his jubilant erection,
then bow down low and kiss the lady's hand.

One sultry Sunday, smoking after lunch,
twelve elder children watched me from their chairs,
the witnesses, crop-haired and flicking ash,

as I tried to ask him questions in bad Czech;
he said nothing that might give himself away;
one answer – *yes* – agreed with all I asked.

So I bribed him with gold packs of cigarettes;
he lit one from the last, his lucky chain;
hands cupped the smoke, still happy, still afraid.

The Disappearing City

The disappearing city in her head
has street names blanked; façades fall to the wind
and cobblestones in waves shine under rain.

One street still stands, and at the top she lives
by a window, closed, unshattered, the last one
of a city of windows waiting for the sun.

Zig-zags where stairs once led. A golden grove
by a black river. Snow falls in the night.
She listens, hunched up in the stony eaves

in company with dragons and angels carved
leaping the walls and arches, their moss eyes
pecked out by all the winter birds she loved

before they flew away. Now her dreaming heart
unlocks its secrets; music, cakes and flowers,
birthdays, deathdays, anniversaries,

the dawn when stormtroops execute the clocks,
and spring, shot in the back, falls down
into a pit of lime, and she wakes blind...

She bolts the door. Liars shout at her
from the next room. The lift whirs up and down
inexplicably, each stop an error.

Phone off the hook; the alarming directories
of a foreign city; a stranger has no name;
the numbers are all wrong; no one is home.

A pillow where her dandelion head
which time has breathed upon, is gently laid
awake and listening to the radio's crack and hiss;

voices, languages, somewhere a lost tune
for chandelier and dancer, long ago;
a midnight waltz, round and around, alone.

To the Partisan Folk Dance Ensemble
of Czechoslovakia

Dear Partisans,
                    the Queen Elizabeth Hall
was barely a quarter-full for your display
of dance and music of the true Slovak.

The compère with her folder and high-heels
explained each song in dictionary terms
of 'circle and digression folk motifs'
and 'tender temperament of boy loves girl'.

Then rings of enamel marionettes burst out
with red, red hearts on sleeves and tongues in cheeks
wound by a key to turn and turn about
while costumed, hatcheted shepherds and recruits

sang shrill and whistled out of jaws wired tight,
and waved them over with the wooing skill
of double-jointed skeletons on strings,
knees up to noses, slapping heels and hearts.

Cellos and fiddles in a music box
bowed up and down in syncopated time
to one old clarinet and a cembalo
played by a boy with Buster Keaton's face.

And one by one the nervous soloists
entered the spotlight circle where they sang
a nursery song in English rendered as
'A little Lambkin has Commenced to Bleat'

while Love in couples through the Harvest Arch
passed out of the pharmaceutical factories,
the sulphur atmosphere, the acid rain,
and into the spring meadows of the song.

Translated to a shadowless stage in the West,
for the dark, empty rows of a concert hall
and the smallest possible audience,
we appreciated the wishing spectacle

which you had studied to restore, revive,
willing time to turn back down the roads
that lead the goose-step soldiers home to bed
and find the old smile on the youngest face.

And at the end applause bought this encore;
like the mechanical figures circling
and waving regal hands and wooden swords
to the toy-time music of Prague's astronomical clock

whose calculated cog-teeth should have struck
blackout midnight in 1968,
the Kings and Queens joined hands, laughed at the joke,
and danced the last dance over once again.

Eureka

Displacing exactly and only yourself
you glissade into the bath; from one angle you look
sunk in a paperweight of glass and quicksilver,
your severed head humming and chatting;
from another your submerged limbs are lensed,
swimming, shoaling. There you lie at rest
in your own star-sign element's
negotiated buoyancy, until you arise,
Mr Venus in your birthday suit
of Saturday morning sunlight,
mortal, guiltless, singing your own fanfare.
Water has no memory,
re-balances inevitably, until
you pull the plug, and shape and volume
diminish like a dying mirror
twisting away down the gargoyle's thirsty throat
to the banshee rattle and bang of the pipes –
enough to raise exactly and only
your displaced absence, your ghost-body, to walk
naked from a source, a stream, a wave,
crying *Eureka!* in the falling rain.

Heaven

(for Mark Willson White, 1957-1994)

The hearse was the mobile flower-bed of his dreams;
gladioli, sunflowers, lilies and orchids bloomed
on polished black, an impossible riot of spring.

They showed us up, shadows in our dark suits
as through North London's traffic we progressed
past the chorus line of incredulous angels

at the bus stop, the shining parade
of shop windows, and the syncopated lights
until we turned down into Jordan Road.

I was a lamentable accompanist
ruining *Nina from Argentina,*
unable to keep time or find the notes;

he'd smile and offer: that was nearly perfect...
I resigned before we made it to the stage.
But as he crossed into the glamour of the lights

in some unlikely basement he was transfigured,
our first angel in sequins and a feather boa
serenading Heaven's glitter-ball.

When the mauve chapel curtains discreetly closed
after the service, for once he did not return
to a standing ovation and an encore –

no *I'll Be Seeing You*, no *Funny Valentine*,
no coloratura aria to his finished body,
achieving that heart-shattering high C:

perhaps we could only hear, or bear to hear
the pitches and the keys of the tuned silence
in which we stood still, waiting,

our flowers set on the ground
that should have been bouquets tossed to the stage
from the footlights as he took his curtain calls.

17

The Story Box
(for Marcel Tohatan)

Created from a plastic yoghourt pot;
rigged up with a radio's spare parts
and hidden beneath a pillow for the secret
story transmitted like the Resistance
in whispers from the improvised kitchen station,
through one thin wall of doubt and interference,
to your sons in bed before they fall asleep
in their high room in a Bucharest tower block.

Perhaps you are still talking to the dark,
almost closing your eyes as you exhale
quixotic smoke into the lamp's angled beam
(coffee and cigarettes your winter fuel),
and tracing the violin curves of your writer's beard;
as if rightly and kindly considering all
the chances of untruthfulness
in those stories they must know by heart.

On a winter night, in a blue-moon light
from the TV's late broadcast of electrical snow,
back in London, simultaneously perhaps,
may I tell your other story? It begins
with my till receipt on which you scribbled
a crazy equation, derived from Einstein's
in a spare hour to prove 'more elegantly'
that time has three dimensions, just like space;

I was drunk with incomprehension,
so you described a grey-walled hotel room;
iron bed, bare window, shadows, no light-bulb;
here two lovers spent one forbidden night;
the moment of truth unzipped beautifully
and unafraid as a summer dress
in a perfect world. But when whatever sun
there was rose in the old Newtonian way

they woke to a collective celebration
outside their window, on an athletics field;
cheerful as revenge, the synchronised
Tractors of Love and Engineers of Souls,
and chanting children schooled in phalanxes;
no birds' aubade, but tannoys shouting out
a crowd countdown against the intimate
silence and rhythm of their last love-making

converting it into a dirty joke.
In your ending they would never meet again;
the woman died, the man lived on at home
with his family in the Bucharest tower block,
talking to the dark, imagining
calculations of impossibility,
primes of lost time, the heart's square root,
its point and infinite recurrences.

'And in the empty room they abandoned hope...'
The two children you have will be asleep
and your desk-lamp in the sky perhaps the last
in the city; between us the insomniac night,
Europe's concrete jigsaw, time- and war-zones;
satellites travel the ether dressed as stars,
their signals tiny pulses, dots and dashes,
becoming tomorrow's weather, the morning news.

Static

When you pulled the t-shirt
over your stooped head
I heard the crackle of static
and imagined the soft,
invisible fur
of charged atmosphere
over the TV's
translucent imagery.

Lights out, my blind
and all-believing hands
discover the ghost
of a smile
on your invisible face;
here you are
in your skin,
shocking against mine.

Small Hours

My grandmother's false teeth are in their glass;
one wall divides her restless sleep from mine
in which I hear her secret nonsense

confessed to the luminous clock face,
each tick a way of knowledge sounding out
the long night with an answer: *it is Christmas*

and you are here again. But this year
may be her last, for look how she has shrunk
into a girl with silver hair

whose own clothes and her exile's history
no longer fit, are strangers' hand-me-downs,
like the English she forgets to speak with me.

This winter reads like her obituary
redeemed in the last line, in which she wakes
in her Prague home lost fifty years away

to crowds and candles in Wenceslas Square,
the paper clocks all set at five to twelve,
and children's children singing *Freedom's Here.*

Her radio broadcasts speeches, bells and hymns
and then the midnight service, *Silent Night*;
trees glittering with angels and snow; bright homes.

Such miracles will not redeem her sense.
Behind the walls our private clocks and hearts
measure the small hours of this dreaming house,

her time now here, now gone with every breath;
odd keys, coat hangers, children's clothes, old soap
laid out for her departure, or for death.

Tonight she hid her teeth beneath the bed;
I rinsed them, wire and plastic in my hand,
and returned them to the language in her head.

Ceausescu's Daughter's Bedroom

Impossible but true;
I am insomniac
in the land of Nosferatu's
spooky dark,

in the silent penthouse
of the Undead;
in Ceausescu's daughter's
shrivelling cold bed.

Her parents were booed
to their rooftop helicopter
by the chanting crowd
in Revolution Square,

then shot by firing squad
on Christmas Day,
their absolute, iconic heads
shown on TV;

abandoned here,
was she the teenage sacrifice
slaughtered by soldiers
for her father's sins,

her only defence
the innocent chocoholic
in the haunted palace
of *realpolitik*?

No one seems to know
the truth of her fate
and much less care. Snow
falls, and I speculate

in her dark chamber which contains
no personal possessions,
but stray bullet-hole burns
in the yellow curtains,

dusty official tomes,
a sixties sunken circle
of seats in crumbling foam,
and a swirly carpet from hell;

no water runs
in these taps at night,
petty tyranny's
B-movie set.

My head on her pillow,
I could almost
pity her,
spoiled ghost

stalking enraged
through the cold tower-blocks
to take her revenge
in bad dreams of sex;

who will not acquiesce
to the stake of light
driven for peace
through her ordinary heart.

Something creaks: the snow, a door;
I switch on the lamp's
small pale against fear
of the dark and sleep;

but no one is there.

Mystery Train

On the Transylvania night train, sixteen coaches long,
a man in denims hand-dyed pollen yellow
played Elvis on his ghetto-blaster as he mimed the words.

He might have glimpsed the King in the fractured glass
of waiting rooms of towns we passed straight through,
transfigured in his rhinestones and great white suit,

so lonely he could die like the last snow
as the mountains melted to the slush of a low dawn
and the train accelerated into silence.

Travelling to a faith healer in the city
without a ticket, at Ploiesti he was turned out
to a waiting crowd and the permafrost of dead loss;

behind him on waste ground a tractor troubled up birds
light as ash in its slow wake. As we pulled away
I looked back at an empty platform of blue smoke;

and when the guard had passed, he reappeared
jubilant in his seat as the long black train
threaded us through the eye of distance into Graceland.

The Juke Box

The place was deserted, the one light stale,
and smelled, like me, of inertia; so, unobserved,
I fed a votive coin to the juke box's steel tongue

and a Wurlitzer rainbow shimmered alive
like the sacred heart of Jesus in a shrine
of tinsel and flock-velvet dark, amen.

Deep in the mechanics, less holy spirits
of punk, jive, salsa, heavy metal, rave,
whirred possessively. What happened next

remains a mystery; I only recall
stylus discovering the acetate spiral,
the nonsense of static, the bony wand of me, and –

imagine, perhaps, a small work of fractal logic,
my random particle as sacred wave,
the Harmony of The Spheres' *All You Need Is Love* –

and then the needle, idling the zero
of the spindle in the after-silence,
and my caught-out heart repeating, repeating,

until something sighed, and was lifted up and away;
the rainbow flickered briefly, and then died;
my coin clattered into the reject tray;

when I fed it back, the b-side began to play.

The Man in the White Suit

Only the light industry of snow
was working in the derelict, curfew city;
a mid-winter night-shift, a hushed revelation
of ice-flowers or flakes of contamination.

We talked about angels: how you needed one
to guard you through these difficult dark days;
you watched as I fell back into a drift
between two cars and waved my arms for wings.

You did not smile. I only made it worse;
as we entered the Hotel Europa's concrete tower
through the revolving door's glass atmospheres,
and the blast of hot air melted everything

I joked I was the man in the white suit
playing cocktail lounge piano, arpeggios,
diminished sevenths, dedicated schmaltz,
serenading you, my Salome;

under the glitter-ball's decadent stars
you'd dance between the tables of businessmen
and currency girls whose shrugged-off furs
hung savage from their chairs; and we'd duet,

the accidental twins of East and West,
crooning each others' secret lives and loves,
the one true poem – but the dazzle stalled
when in perfectly bladed English you replied:

This is the new Europa of Yes or No,
of night-life, gambling and pornography,
luxury, uncertainty and despair;
of accusation and idealisation,

revenge and freedom and the gods'
bargains of the chances of a lifetime.
This is my prison; but you just play along
like Liberace, chronic and naïve.

And so how candidly you set my head
on its tarnished platter, my idiotic talk
stopped with a joke-apple garnishing
my gob-smacked jaw. Then you were going,

going, in the taxi's porphyry and rust;
you looked out at my snow and nailed it *slush,*
too wet to bear the image of anything;
and then the door slammed and you sped away

between the pot-holes, monuments and icy works
of your dark city, leaving me alone
in the revolving door, my fragile crown
and white suit melting on me where I stood.

Icons

On Sunday morning couples are strolling,
footsteps in time, long shadows converging,
up the boulevards towards the park.

Horia Gerbea is our tour-guide;
he points out the pockmarked garden and villa walls
where the fighting was fierce by the TV centre,

the tarpaulin shroud on the National Library,
and the remains of little shrines to the memory
of girls in high heels run down by tanks.

At the boating-lake, drained to a tundra of ice,
wrapped figures sit with fishing sticks
and the tenure of history; behind them,

the House of the People's fondant-white façades,
Ceausescu's final *folie de grandeur*;
a thousand empty marble and concrete rooms

built on a dozen churches, three monasteries,
and seven thousand homes. Too many windows
fuse the sun's gold patina like an icon.

He poses against it for a photograph,
imperious, impeccable, amused;
poet and softcore pornographer,

founder of the Party of Free Love,
ghost-writer of the first sex newspaper
and a story on the lone ticket collector

who fined fare-dodgers at the end of the line
a blow-job at the back... This dextrous bluff
was his favourite apocrypha until

a deputation armed with baseball bats
from the Ticket Collectors' Union came for him
and forced him to recant such heresy.

He takes a bow, then smiles, then gently shrugs
the "innocent" gesture with his empty hands –
a stand-up in the junta of revenge.

Chocolate and Salt

When Prague was given to Hitler she packed
just crystal, photographs, and a cookery book
for London's unfurnished accommodation.

What fell into the silence in her head
were the doodlebugs, their sudden candlelights
illuminating the black-out every night.

What could be taken from her was not hers,
so gifts and wishes are never to be trusted;
toasters, cameras, kettles, and gramophones

are locked away in the wardrobe whose mirror-door
shows an old woman carefully turn the key.
We sing her *Happy Birthday*, tuneless and slow.

Now make a wish and blow the candles out;
we make her mutter and pretend to know
the secret which, confessed, will not come true,

but holds us here together once a year
around her table, staring at the salt
in its tiny cellar of Bohemian glass,

our silence and her story in the sharp
tang of every pinch of flavouring
of exile in her bones-and-water soup.

A chicken carcass, chocolate cake and salt;
three empty places (we are gone again);
the wishbone in two pieces on her plate.

Tonight she will be waiting in the dark,
her savings stitched into her winter coat,
for the night journey through the mirror door

where we are hiding with our surprise gifts
of chocolate hearts and wishbones, shadows and salt;
and in the hollow wood wire hangers chime.

The General at the Bus Stop

The General settles down to wait for dawn
in his office on the pavement. Soon the first
bus rounds the dark corner of the road,
all lights on, packed with sleepers. Travelling
is not his nature, whose four legs sustain
an early tour around the square's best haunts
(church steps, stone fountain, kiosk, café chairs),
and carry his slow shadow on his back
across the street at noon to pass the time.
His colleague in indifference is that old
devil the station master, tortured by
a timetable that wakes him like a fool
to the last star and in dead afternoons.
The buses never come or go on time
but vanish with the travellers,
their luggage, money, perfume, stories, shoes,
with tickets to the cities or the sea,
or healers in the mountain villages;
as his family abandoned him
to the ravings of an under-table world,
who once walked on his hind legs and shook hands.

Last Train

A woman dressed in all her wardrobe plays
a comb cadenza; she has packed her bags
into bags, a Circle Line refugee.

At her feet a handful of spare change
cast heads or tails with the useless foreign tender:
an ear of wheat, a leaping fish, the wrong Queen.

North

The article on tectonics proposed
an original green world
where oranges ripened
in the Arctic's sunny fields.

If you believe the evidence –
the fossils of sunflowers
shading reclining mammoth bones –
paradise was everywhere.

Lying here side by side,
where in the world are we?
Snake shadows on the bed,
mad game shows on late-night TV,

and London like a juggernaut,
its lights a cargo of oranges
driving north across the night's
deep-frozen lake, a new ice age.

The Very Rich Hours

(for Dave Royle, 1960-1996)

His window frames our pictured, distanced city:
people, traffic, countless other windows,
the very rich hours of the land of the living.

Inside the golden sun illuminates
four vases of flowers, a plastic water-jug,
dust motes in the vacancy, and Dave in a red chair.

I sit facing his level, absent gaze
the muscles of anger and pleasure have withered to;
he does not know me: I hardly know him.

Each morning he is cradled in a bath;
his cigarettes burn down to his finger-tips;
all I can do for him is tap the ash.

Pitched against the gym's weights and measures,
discovered in the fluencies of the showers,
his body seemed to me a worked perfection;

he used it for spare cash and for the stories;
up cranky Soho stairwells, in gas-fire rooms
he modelled for "amateur photographers"

who tested him up close with their light meters,
and composed him – athletic, classical –
held still, *'Poetry!'*, for their camera fire.

Between a bureau de change and a cigarette kiosk
he'd return to London's arcane A-Z
of night life, bars, punters, strangers and friends;

there were dark back-rooms and moonless midnight parks,
shadows in the margins, the casual glory of skin;
desire, not the sorrow of desire.

Now mortality has become familiar;
his friends are dying, or gathered here, or both,
in this book of hours and hours of smoking and waiting

to turn the page; and nothing to be done
except to stay, so simple and difficult. Leaving,
I picture him for the last time, for myself;

his window discloses a dark, deserted city;
the traffic lights are changing on their own;
the moon repeats itself in countless windows.

The silenced TV casts its blue and silver,
the world's text, irrelevantly across
the parchment of his dream-skin;

the tattoed swallow soars from his right arm
and his slight weight; may tomorrow's sunlight
shine right through to illuminate his heart:

a Proper of Time, a brief history, a love story.

Art and Mystery
(for Andrew Wood, 1944 – 1993)

> *'Art and mystery: a formula employed in indentures
> binding a craftsman to a trade.'*
> OXFORD ENGLISH DICTIONARY

Transformations were the mystery of his craft,
exigencies the occasion of good work;

so his last commission, a stage design, revealed
a mural of paradise graffitoed on a wall,

which could open to a suburb of sound-effects
or dissolve into the glass periphery

and pent waves dancing of a swimming pool;
all realised in plywood, paint and light.

By then he could not walk, his sight was bad,
and night by night his indentured body taught

its arts and mysteries, to be learned by rote, by heart;
long lists of pills and pains, t-cells and trials,

symptoms and signs, no act, his own blue eyes
in the shaving-mirror's face of inlayed bones

seeing the shadow of his own elegy; and then
the morning lights came up and he was gone.

This last scene was still his, designed for us:
our flowers and candles, our luck in continuing;

the back-stage crew nonchalantly prepared
to strike his coffin to the exit-state of fire;

and *I'm Going Home* from *The Rocky Horror Show*
playing us out through the open chapel doors

to talk of his good dying, and smiles of grief;
to roses, lawns, green trees, and people slowly walking.

I thought of the famous sofa he'd devised;
worked by hydraulics, it slowly carried him

along his balcony of roses and bamboos,
propped up in stately progress through the day

staying in the sun of his last spring.
In that light anything seemed possible:

the sofa levitating on mysterious thermals
and a harmonic hum of his own invention

into thin air, the blue, a dazzled nowhere.
But the park bench I sat on would not budge an inch.

The Cure

Not the laying-on of hands, healing bones and hearts.
Not flowers, protease inhibitors, pills for the pain.
Not a prayer for the dying, for you, for us, not crying, not yet.

Tonight only the clock, each concentrated second one tiny grain
in a thousand thousand parts
of rain.

Dunes

Your heart is more complicated
than the coastline of Norway;
but then you decide to describe
a place you had forgotten
until this moment, a secret beach
discovered by luck or chance,
the long curved shore exactly answering
to the description of the waves,
a far echo of Atlantic ultramarine, salt and glitter
returning home at last
just as you say: *There we could be*
nudists nesting in a sand dune's heat and hush
of two freak waves in step
that cancel each other out
as if the sea stood still and listened
for one strange moment
to the truth;
afterwards, on tide-ribbed sand we'd find
six eggs unbroken in a box,
a cornelian the colour of the light,
and a milk-carton from Quebec.

The Single Shoes of Spain

The bridge is the gypsies' ceiling; every summer
they travel to the stones of this dry river
with the rag and bone of all the family
and set up residence, no door, no key.
The men stand at the bar; the women wash
the clothes, and lay them out on a thorn bush
or the hot stones, then retire to the shade
to watch them dry. They have no money; trade
is what the river gives away, the scrap
the wealthy town dumps off the bridge. Cars drop
broken on the rocks; cookers, burnt out,
a red armchair, some prams, a plastic bucket,
a doll's head, an umbrella. And the shoes,
the single shoes of Spain, those mysteries
of slipper, boot, stiletto without a pair,
useful only to the lottery-ticket seller
with two left feet, or a dancer with one leg;
eyes lacking laces, soles all broken tongues.
September, they move on to the winter bridges,
leaving some shoes, and several empty fridges.

Ice Cream

The railways feed their tracks into King's Cross.
Fluorescent lemons and foil in the all-night stores,

one to cut, the other to fashion
the packets, exchanged by mouth:

that deep kiss, a moment of business;
her parting face like ice-cream in winter.

Ausonius and Paulinus

(for Peter Hobson, d. December 1995)

Born in Aquitaine, A.D. 353;
tutor to Gratian, the Emperor's son;
rewarded with the office of High Consul;
a millionaire, he retires to his estates in Bordeaux.

Barbarian degeneration on every frontier;
their appalling taste in music, trousers and hair-grease;
a boom and bust economy, temple treasury gold
flooding the market; time's harvest rotting in the streets...

Thankful for his last brilliant apt pupil,
the sweet embodiment of the old world;
Pontius Paulinus, who speaks flawless Latin,
whose career at twenty-one outshines his teacher's.

Then married, he disappears into Spain.
Three years of silence. Finally he writes,
a Christian convert and a father grieving
the death of his only child, *refusing what may be seen*

to reach what may not be seen. Ausonius,
now seventy, composes his last letter
beseeching him to come before he dies.
His pupil sends these line as his reply:

I, through every mortal fate or chance,
however long my skin imprisons me,
across the whole world's hopeless distances,
will call to mind and heart each part of you,

not in silence, not with downcast face,
but as if your flesh were knit into my flesh,
the very thought of you seen with my eyes,
instant, present, vision true as flesh.

And when I die and rise to the next world,
the heavenly universe of stars and light,
I will not cease to think, as in this world,
of you in everything, becoming light

as love leaving the ruins of the heart,
returning to its immortality,
yet looking back, unable to forget
you remembered in eternity.

But Paulinus did not come. He too died old,
priest of the shrine of St Felix in Nola,
composing verse and sweeping dust and leaves
from the threshold every day into the sun.

Dr Johnson's Bicycle

Balance
is the impossible
baffling trick
like luck
which comes at once
or not at all
true as the whistle
of a blackbird
in the leaves
before flying
into its element
of silence

and skaters
circling
backwards
while at the brink
of the rink
couples
on knife blades
negotiate
the uncertain
scribbled
palimpsest
of ice

Dr Johnson's
bicycle
a metaphysical
contraption of iron
which puzzled
he thought you must
both ride
and simultaneously
ride yourself
making sense of faith
and nonsense
of science

the cogs and works
of a travelling clock
whirling out
from the still
chained
hub of Love
through palindrome spokes
to the relative
perpetuum mobile
of a wheel
turning the world's
transience

and the infinite
possibilities
of a puncture
coming down
a panoramic pass
in a rainstorm
when the front wheel
comes suddenly
free and runs
bucklingly on
before losing its way
in the distance

while I
fail to escape
the sudden
screaming
joke bone-
shaker crash
or shape my fall
as a light
leap
to the hard ground
of common
sense

Six Studies of Anna Vondraček

I

Dressed up for a sitting with Rembrandt
in a stranger's velvet coat and old fox fur
tatty from the wars, her self-portrait
shows two old ladies, both as amateurs
in the confusing art of light and shade;
one's waiting in the station booth's black box
and daydreaming inside the shuttered eye;
the other, surprised by the stark flash, thinks
the moment gone, moves, and is next caught, blurred,
leaving the booth – and history – goodbye!

II

The Club of Amateur Photographers
of Prague recorded odder local tales;
tightrope walkers crossing a town square;
balloonists, unicyclists; ghosts; and girls
in flowerbed hats; the negative white
winter bones beneath the summer skin;
and here's a wedding day, the child-bride
clutching a chaplet and her next-of-kin;
two formal sitters in the cold northlight
beneath a roof of glass, with no background.

III

There are no photographs of her war years:
'Packing in a hurry, 1939',
unsmiling for the last time at the front door;
leaving from the Hlavni railway station,
not posed like a film-star at the carriage window
bound for Hollywood's technicolour future,
no sudden confetti of flashlights
or crowds waltzing towards departures
beneath the mirror-ball of history
as all her flowers are turned to black and white.

IV

Later, the multiple instamatic copies
of her summer holidays in Majorca
when she is alone in her mid-sixties,
asking anyone at all to take her picture;
a sequence in the hotel swimming pool,
in her pink glasses and the plastic flowers
of her bathing hat, a retired Aphrodite
treading the glitter of held-still waters;
then several of the empty swimming pool;
and of the empty chair she sat in by the sea.

V

Every year she stood by the Christmas tree's
winking lights and unbalanced fairy,
equally dressed in borrowed finery,
grasping my brother and me, and a sweet sherry.
With her gifts unopened in their wrapping paper
on Boxing Day we drove her back to London
cruel in the frost; up in the night
at her high window she waved until we were gone,
holding the curtains open like a camera's shutter,
crying for more time, and for more light.

VI

Here she is lastly, taken as a child
in a photographer's *atelier*
at an old biplane's controls, the bold
aviator (watching at her shoulder
a guardian pigeon) high above the still,
painted streets of Prague, set to depart
on her solo voyage far away from home;
no wind in her white curls or tighter heart,
and waving like an uncertain angel;
then lost in the clouds' silence and slow time.

The Space Race

When astronauts touched down in the Sea of Tranquility,
took one small step, and fixed the Stars and Stripes,
my father cried; I watched him from my window
in his summer garden, staring at the moon.

This was the suburbs; one family quintet
played Beethoven and ate bagels for tea;
another dressed in visors and silver suits
waved as they strolled down to the shuttered hives.

For him our green-belt peace was the Cold War
by other means; Brezhnev and Nixon
conducted their kitchen debates around our table;
guttural aliens from Mars

plotted to destroy democracy;
his back lawn was mown in longitudes
like theoretical shadows of fallout;
our own détente deteriorated into silence...

But for that last lap of the space race
we shared the odyssey's home-movie together:
the Eagle's wire, tin and silver foil
like a home-made family car, the two astronauts'

giant, dreamy steps in gardens of dust
on holiday from gravity, the sky
always black, and over the white horizon
our blue and perfect world hung in the night.

My paperback time-travellers were lost,
dividing and vanishing improbabilities
miscalculated simultaneously
like swimmers in the pool's wavelengths of light,

like me, the visitor returning home;
the sprinkler still repeats its radar arc
but my mother's dead, strangers are neighbours,
and I step towards my father

thirty years ago standing alone
in bright light on his perfect, pyrrhic lawn,
whose greatest wish was a ticket to the moon;
who waters his garden by the summer stars.

In Memory of Vincent Cox
(born Lambeth 1923, died Harpenden 1991)

(for Iain Cox)

Who loved the knack of luck, of stakes and odds,
an ace, seven sevens, a hole in one;

who disappeared on Saturday afternoons
through the forbidden ribbon door

of the obscure betting shop, to reappear
hours later in his old leather armchair,

smiling his winnings, smoking, drinking tea
by the potful, and watching the TV.

Who loved to fly, Lancasters, a bomber's moon
on midnight raids, on Dresden in '45,

the figurine homes, churches, the platz and parks
razed, each family walking shades

where china turned to ash, and tears to salt,
glass buckled, light went blind, the phosphorus heart

crazed; who still came home against the odds
in a plane he called Mizpah ('In God we Trust').

Who traded his wings in post-war civvy street
for a wife and son, the green-belt, a salesman's car

and business travelling north to Staffordshire's
bleak pottery furnaces and crucibles;

who loved the lucent angles and singing rim
of cut-glass fluted on the blowing rod

from a bulb of light; sand, potash, lime,
oxides and carbonates, transfigured to

an affluence of decanters and services,
pastoral figures on the mantlepiece,

an attic of first editions packed in straw
for his after-life, and two porcelain

lucky angels cool in his left hand
as the right turned aces up or cast the dice.

Who watched with us on winter afternoons
the Sunday war film, equally black and white;

clipped, self-effacing, nonchalant braveries,
one engine spluttering, impossibly

homing on a wing and a prayer
to the orchestra's finale and dawn's light.

Who crash-landed in his armchair, years later,
the guilty survivor when his wife had gone

and neither luck nor prayer could win her back;
whose photograph would never speak, however

long he stared, sat in the early dark
among unwashed teacups and full ash-trays

losing the slow day's games of Patience.
Who carefully washed the cups, tidied the house,

smoked his last cigarette, pencilled a note
on the back of an envelope, and then

bailed out of the attic's small trap-door
into the hall's sudden January light.

Who played the joker, but who was not this;
the undertaker's mistaken parting

running through his hair on the wrong side,
a cotton smile on his face as if he might

rise to greet us, Lazarus at his wake,
and still believe himself to be blessed by luck.

Whom I last remember as a window ghost
in his living room reflected in the night

on an incandescent lawn of December frost,
ironing his white shirts in an empty room.

Whose older brother told a better winter's tale;
White City dog track, winter '33;

mother, the infamous gambler who seems
to have wagered and lost her husband in a bet,

was having a run of bad luck, but staked her last
(their return tube fare) in a four-dog race

on the outside track; gates up, the inside three
collide and knock each other cold,

while Outside Chance raced on under the lights
to an illuminated victory

at hopeless-to-one; which brought for Wally and Vince
a slap-up tea and a taxi home to bed.

Who was released out of a winter day,
his secrets, wishes and excuses turned to ash

while we stood in his absence, uncertain
tick-tack men signing *goodbye, goodbye*

to a lucky man who seemed to lose himself
and his laughter; a chancer of odds, grounded,

who loved to fly, the navigator
over enemy country, charts and compasses,

flight angles and lucky angels, blessed wings,
seeking the constant, simple, bright North Star

in the night sky he knew by heart.
Iain, do you remember how we'd play

for coppers or matchsticks when we were kids,
your father deftly shuffling the pack?

Who might forgive – with the grace of his good luck,
with the ghost of a chance – these words as my low stake

raised against loss and in his memory,
though I can find no words to say to you.

The Angel of History

This is the door I've knocked at all my life;
been quizzed for my name and the family shibboleths
before three bolts are drawn, and I go in.

Now here we stand, my father, my brother, me,
her three men in a row. Inside we find
the scene of a crime, an accident, a wrong;

sour milk, an unwashed cup, a tarnished spoon
fallen to the floor, one tap's slow drip
scaling the turquoise enamel of the basin;

and there on the floor charred bolts of her night-dress
scattered like feathers from the angel of history
on fire in a spontaneous last waltz.

She lived for two more weeks in a white ward bed,
weird as Lear, throwing her tea at the wall,
the confessions of her chattering false-teeth

smothered beneath the pillow, while her own words
lost their way in a mouth too soft and old
to enunciate the brilliance of the joke.

She laughed and laughed. I stood like Harpo, dumb,
and stroked her hair, not touched with love for years,
until she drifted off with a ceasing sigh;

but as soon as I tried to tiptoe away, she was up,
wide awake, contradictory, wronged, peeling bandages
to expose the unredeemable skin of her agony.

Her story ends in this padlocked hoard of clocks,
paper money, postcards, a scratched LP of Strauss,
the smallest articles in which she could keep faith;

I find my birth recorded in her diary's
inimitable shorthand: 'Boy born. Shopping. Tea':
more words of hers than she ever read of mine.

On the inside of the door she had pinned a sign:
DO NOT OPEN. For the last time we pull it shut,
and my father drops her keys back through the letter box.

The Ghost Train

Along the esplanade the season's last
empty deck-chairs recline to catch the rain
to the starboard of a café steaming up.

The donkeys leave their circle in the sand;
the fortune-teller closes up her shrine;
the floral clock can wither to its sticks.

Patience and pebbles, tea-leaves and cigarettes;
between the window and mirror winter steams.
Dried flowers in the grate, rain at the pane

where Mr Blatný scribbles poetry,
sheet after sheet in his own language lost
each day the forty years since he was wrecked

on this asylum island where he found
a beach of unmarked sand, drank tea from urns,
and rode the ghost train round and round and round

A Cookham Sunday

'The holy suburb of Heaven'
STANLEY SPENCER

In Spencer's final pencil-ghosted canvas
Christ preaches at the Cookham Regatta
not to the posh in punts with Chinese lanterns
but to a boy perched on a rib of the horse-ferry,
amazed by the spade-bearded loony's story
of the resurrection of the dozy dead
on Sunday morning, yawning from their stone beds;
he sketched them from this bridge above the river,
but the scene was already gone, like the commuting gents:
survivors, mostly, from the Armistice,
on high summer mornings in the thirties
they'd slough dark suits, leave neat black shoes and socks
in little piles along the bank
and dive in, white as the Cookham swans.

At Boulter's Lock in 1968
my mother takes a maiden drive alone
in her brand-new chrome-and-white Triumph Herald;
lipstick-check, sunglasses, cigarette,
she finds first gear, frees the brake, throws me a wave,
smiles into the blue beyond of the windshield
in heaven with the freedom, and pulls out
on the river's traffic of tricks where she moves
hardly at all, then changes gear, accelerates
up the razzle-dazzle of the current
(I'd call *that's the wrong way*, I'd shout *come back*)
until her wing-mirrors' sudden clap of light
– two doves – and through the sorry weir's
drawn curtains she vanishes.

Spencer's left his pitch with the pram of paints,
but the gazing day stays broad and still,
and I'm my mother's age then, now,
staring spellbound from the steps – mine too,
the very eyes of the children's audience
for whom the river's secret gears still raise

the pleasure boats and their lucky families
blinking on the generous water
with 99s whorled like torches in their hands
to the putative cries of laughter and music; then
the lock-gates collar-bones swing gently open
releasing each one up the shining level
against the current of the afternoon
to the sunlight's congregated *dot dot dot*...

The Foley Artist

'A specialist in creating sounds, especially of body movement,
recorded to fit the pictures on the screen'
THE COMPLETE FILM DICTIONARY

A strange calling; to play the minor effects,
the off-screen score you notice by its absence;
but in this small suitcase of tricks I hold
the bricabrac of people being there,
the world dismantled to its sticks and stones.
For instance; I can conjure my own approach
from foggy distances with a handful of pebbles;
the swish of corduroy, the creak of leather
are just two of several variations
played upon fine ribbons of sandpaper.
Paper torn is fire; an ounce of sand
hissing in a matchbox is the sea,
or the Sahara, or a deep sleep.
A mirage of ice is done with ice and glass.
Ten raindrops caught in zero gravity
can be a storm. A grain of salt is tears.
I could articulate the life and death
agonies of a snowflake, or this my grin.
With ebony, feathers, needles, smoke and dust
I have mastered all the little noises of war.
It is my music. Time is two tin hands,
one all-purpose twinkling tinsel star,
a splinter of moon-rock, and its tidal pull:
breath-mist fading on an inch of mirror.
Mystery is velvet, silver nitrate night.
Imagine me, now, alone in my dark room,
no words, no music, and no audience;
a hyperactive, lunatic one-man band
working to the speed of shadow and light,
tinkling, jingling, rattling, scratching, banging
from small Genesis to minor Apocalypse;
but I do the last frames like a dream:
a question mark, a balloon twisted awry;
a football rattle cranked; stopped with a nail;
and last the great arcana of smoke-rings

to create the loop-hole through which I disappear
as if I was never here.

And so this is the end; and please remember:
a slamming door is always a slamming door.

NOTES

Ivan Blatný was born in Brno in 1919. At the end of the 1940s he defected while visiting London. After a breakdown he lived in institutions for the rest of his life, lastly in Clacton on Sea. He was remembered in Prague when Vaclav Havel, who was a fan, became President. Blatný died in 1990; a bumper volume, *Verse 1933-53*, has been published in Prague, but not yet translated.

Anna Vondraček was born in Prague in 1904, left for London in late 1938, and died in 1992.

**Indianapolis
Marion County
Public Library**

Renew by Phone
269-5222

Renew on the Web
www.imcpl.org

For general Library information
please call 269-1700.